# I Do Not Want To Take A Nap

**by Cassie Lindblom**

**Illustrations by Robin Cain**

I Do Not Want To Take A Nap

Copyright © 2024 by Cassie Lindblom

All rights reserved. No part of this book may be reproduced or transmitted in any form or by any means without written permission of the author.

ISBNs:
979-8-9900461-0-8 (paperback)
979-8-9900461-1-5 (hardcover)
979-8-9900461-2-2 (eBook)

Library of Congress Control Number: 2024904946

Published by Lindblom Books
Chaska, Minnesota

For Silas, I love you forever!
~Cassie

To my husband Phil and my sons,
Riley, Christian, Ashton, and Nathan.
~ Robin

I do not want to take a nap.
No nap for me today!

There is no time for sleeping,
all I want to do is play.

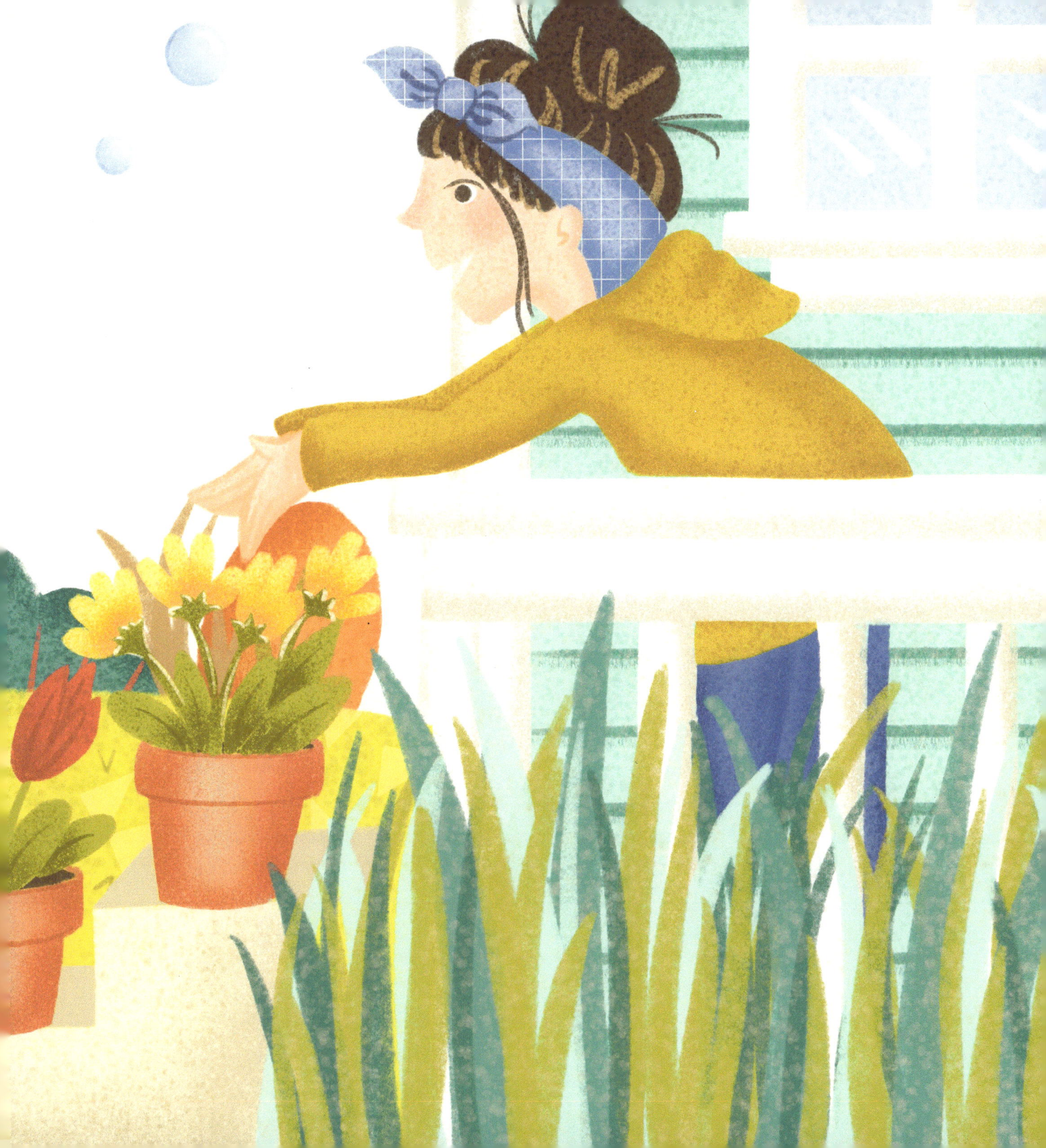

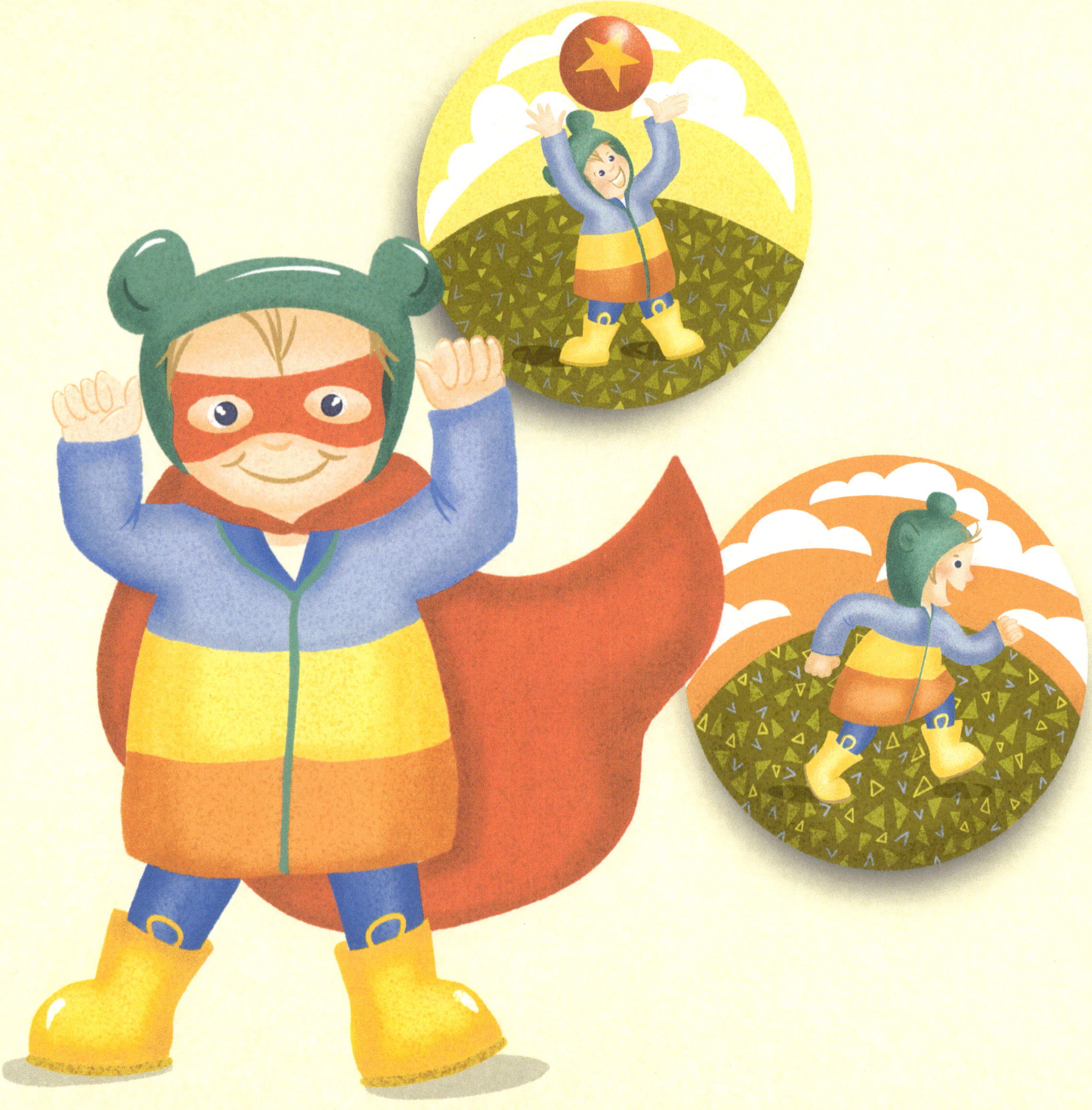

I'm not even tired,
watch and see
what I can do.

I can dance and
jump and run,
just to name a few.

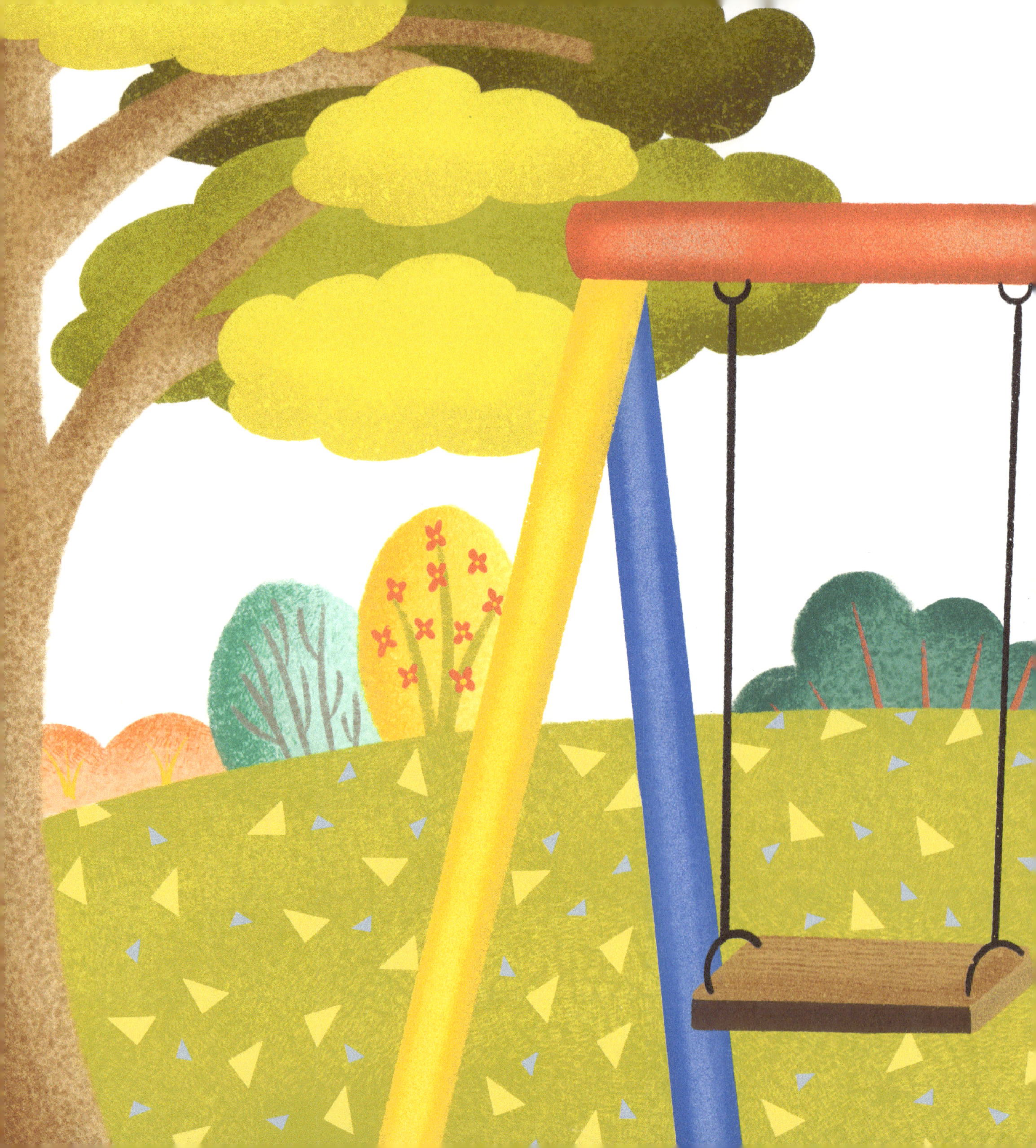

I see that you are having fun and do not want to quit.
Your body will say thank you if you rest it for a bit.

Playing hard like you do takes lots of energy.

Let's go pick out some books. We'll read them, you and me.

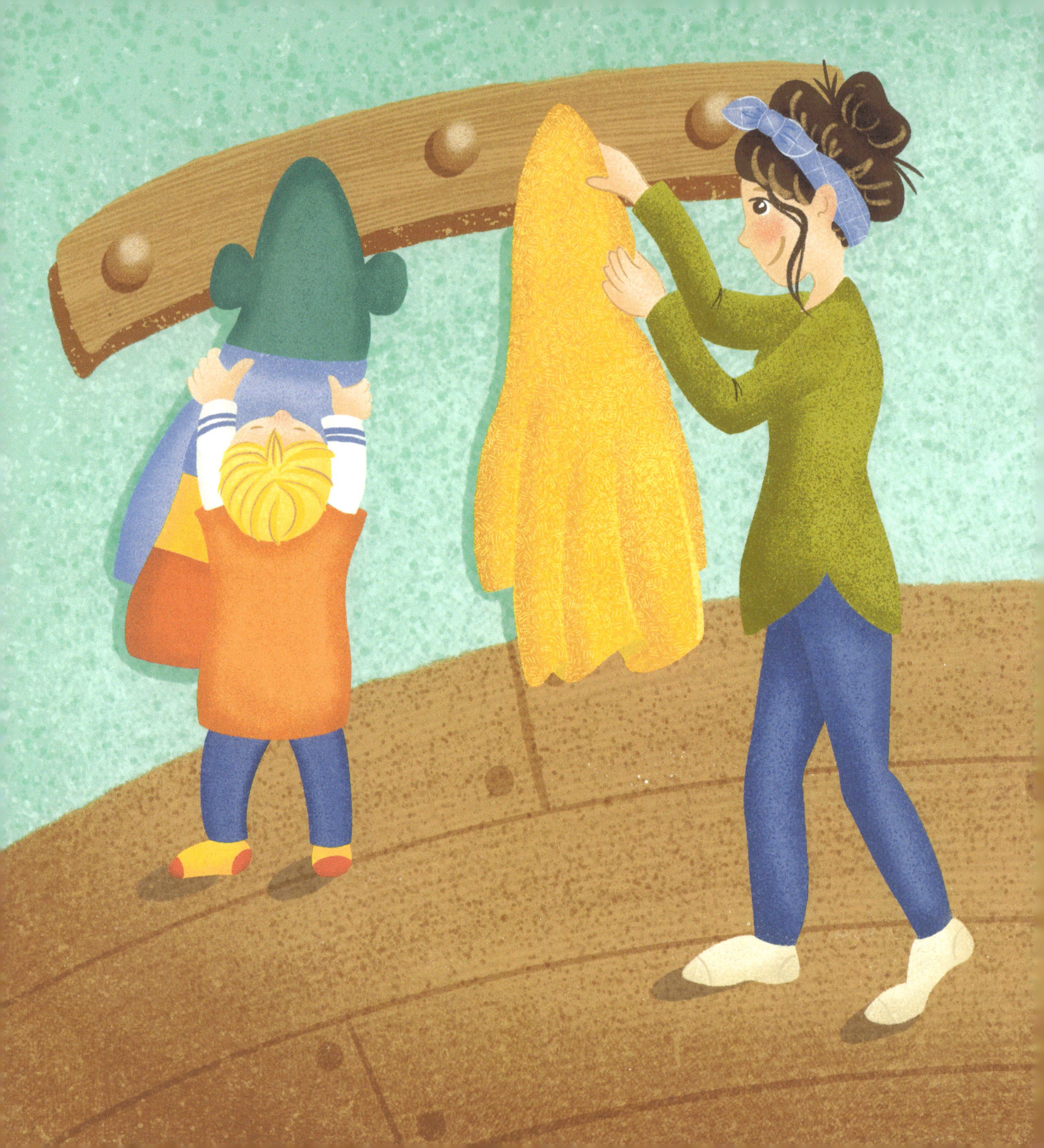

You know how much I love to read,
I can't say "no" to that.

But just a couple, then it's back
to climbing on my mat.

Come on up and sit with me.
We'll cuddle in your chair.

Here's your blanket,
don't forget to grab
your teddy bear.

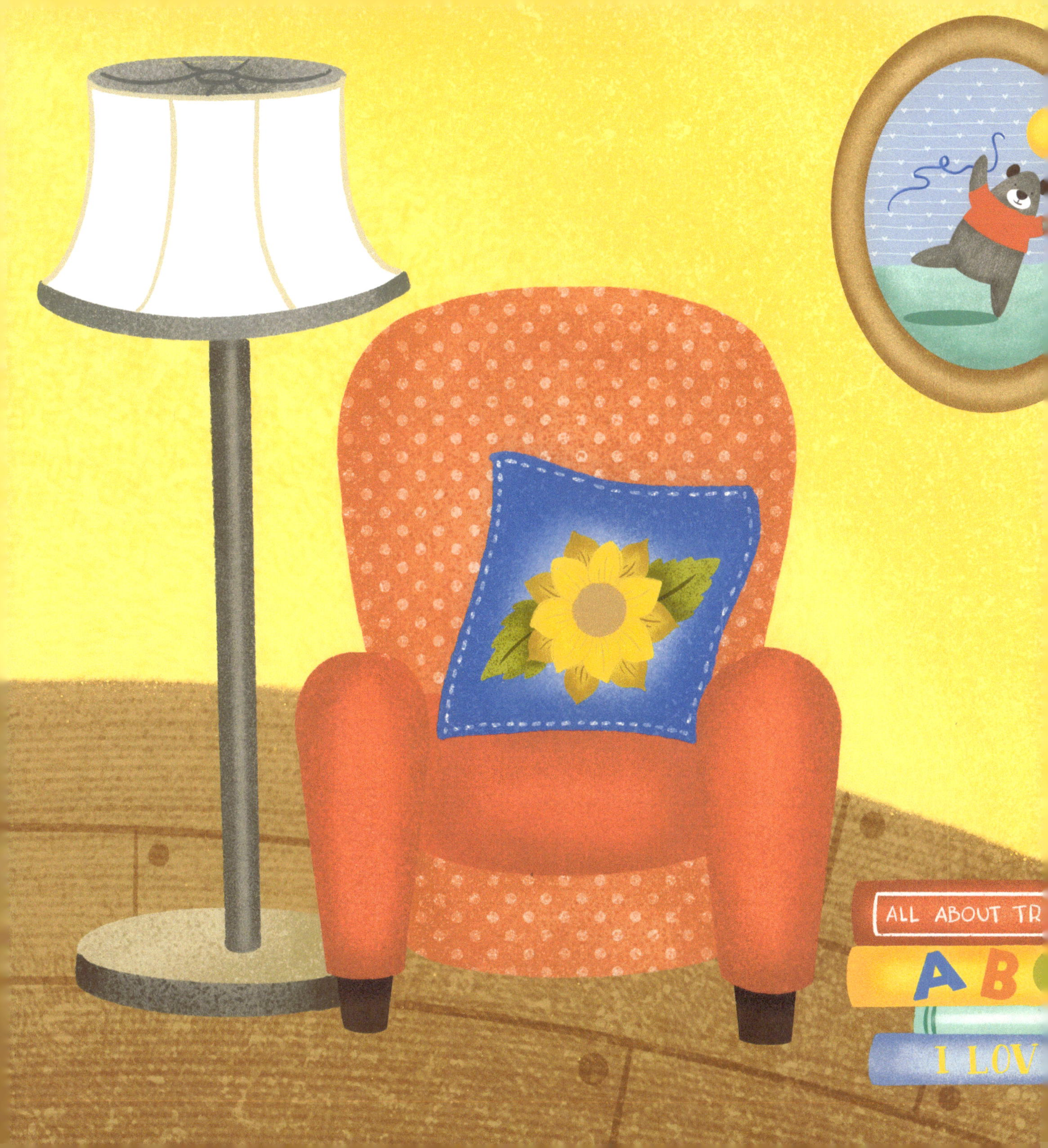
ALL ABOUT TR
ABC
I LOV

Just so you know, I'm on to you,
I see right through your ways.

You're hoping that these books
will put me in a sleepy daze.

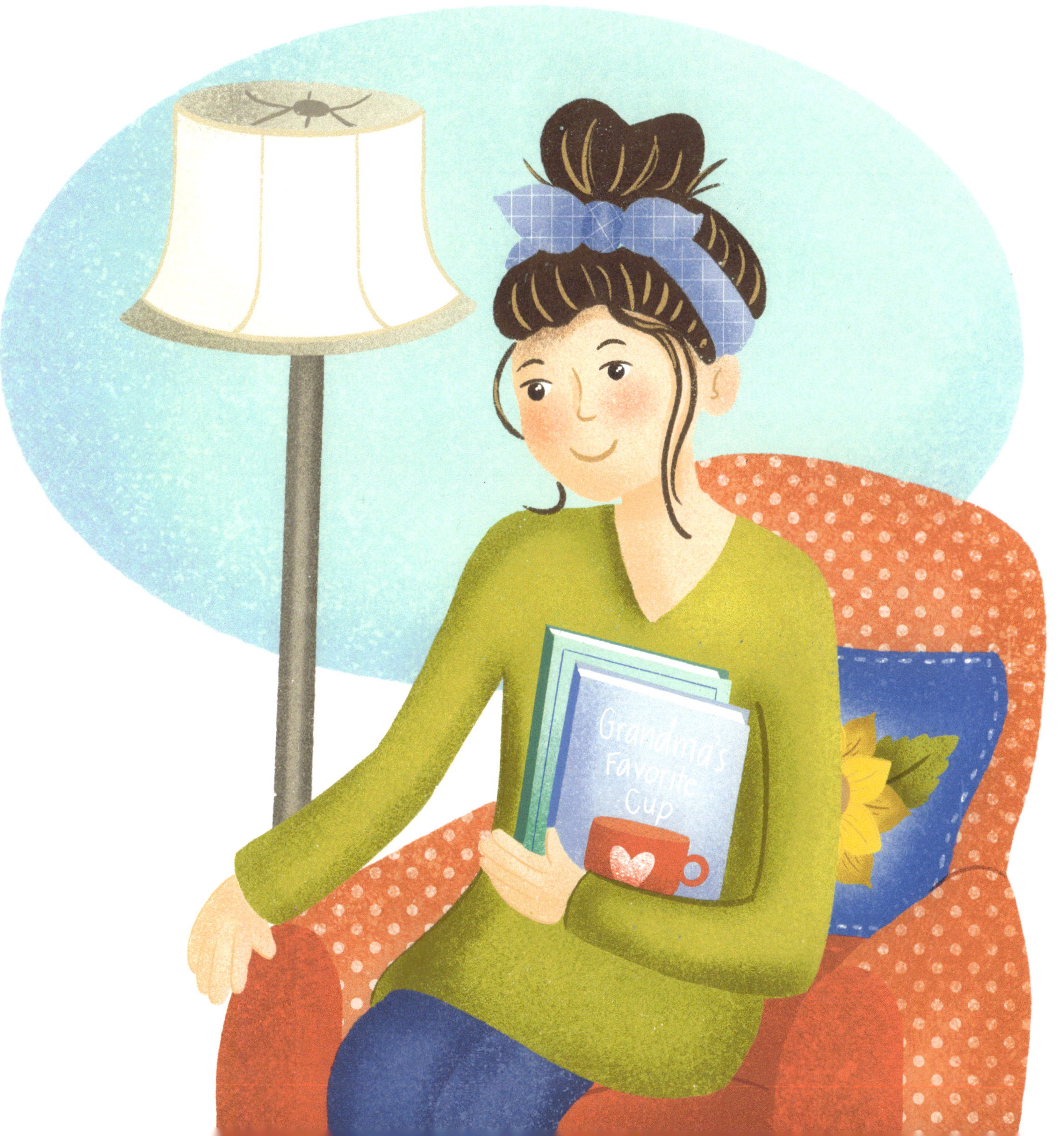
Grandma's Favorite Cup

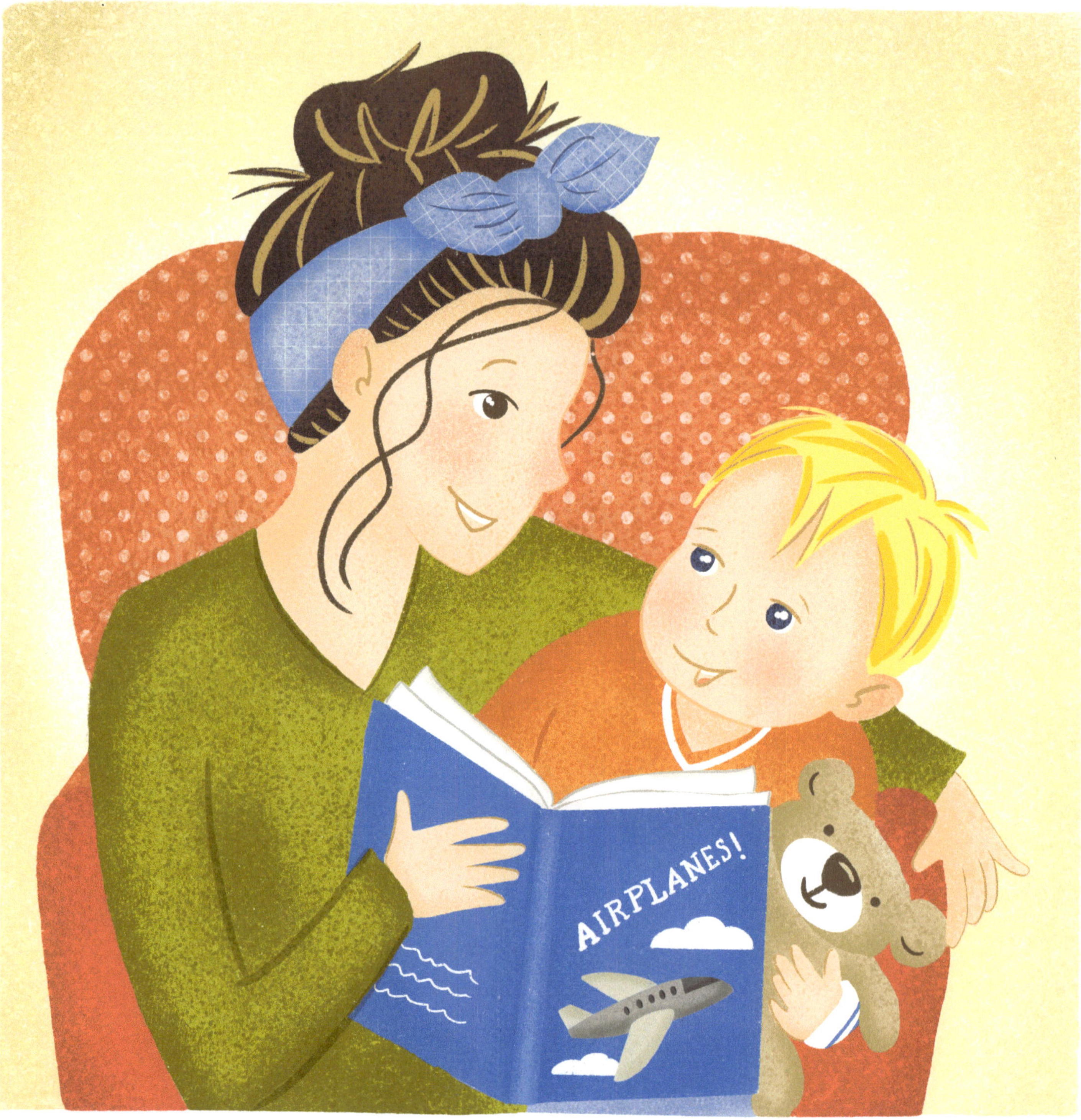
AIRPLANES!

And while I might feel warm and snuggly,
Sitting on your lap,
There is no way, now hear me say,
"I will not take a nap!"

It's okay if you can't sleep,
and all you do is rest.

All I ask is you lie down and truly try your best.

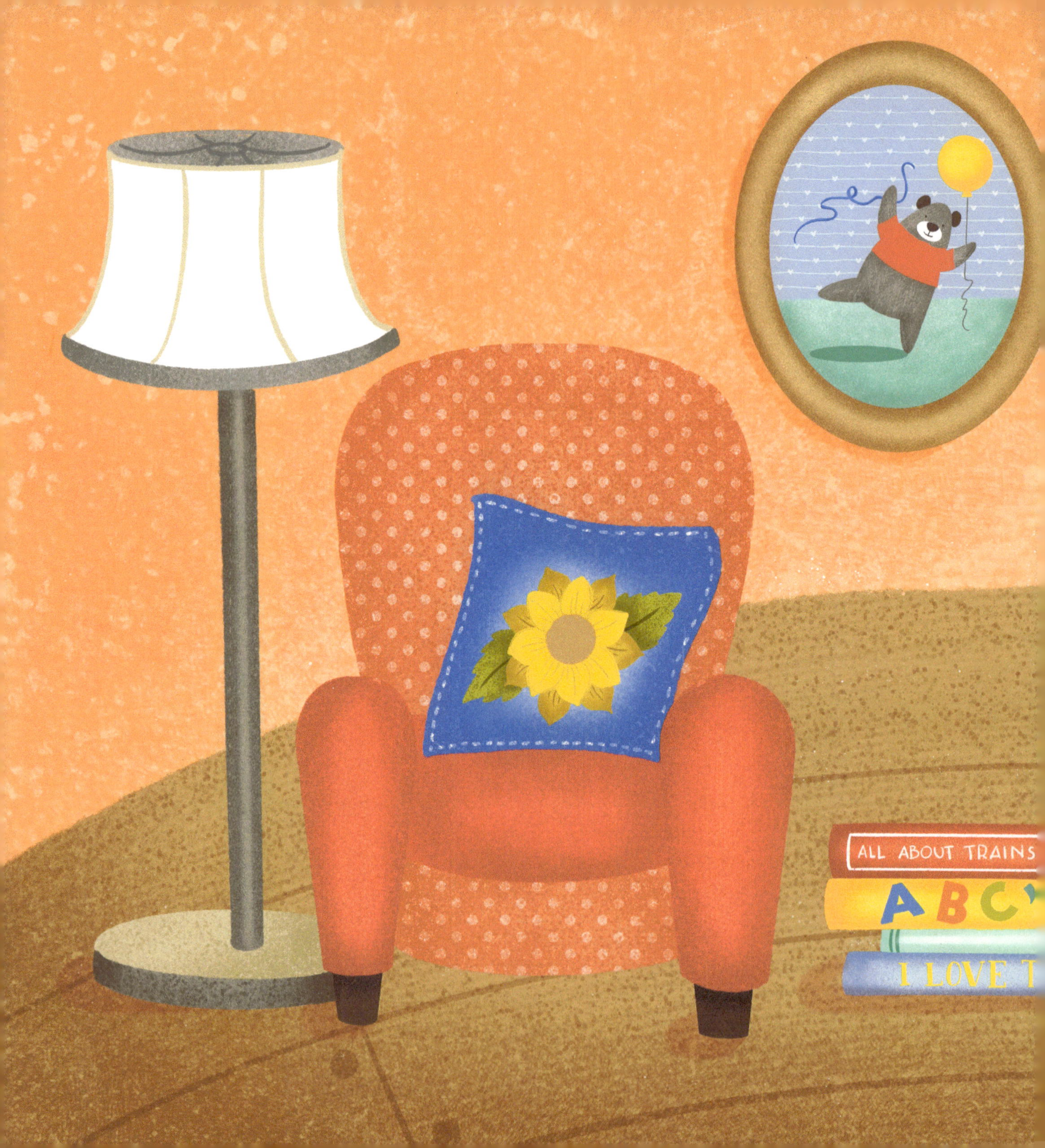
ALL ABOUT TRAINS
ABC
I LOVE T

Let's get you comfy in your bed. It doesn't hurt to try.

I'll even rub your back and sing your favorite lullaby.

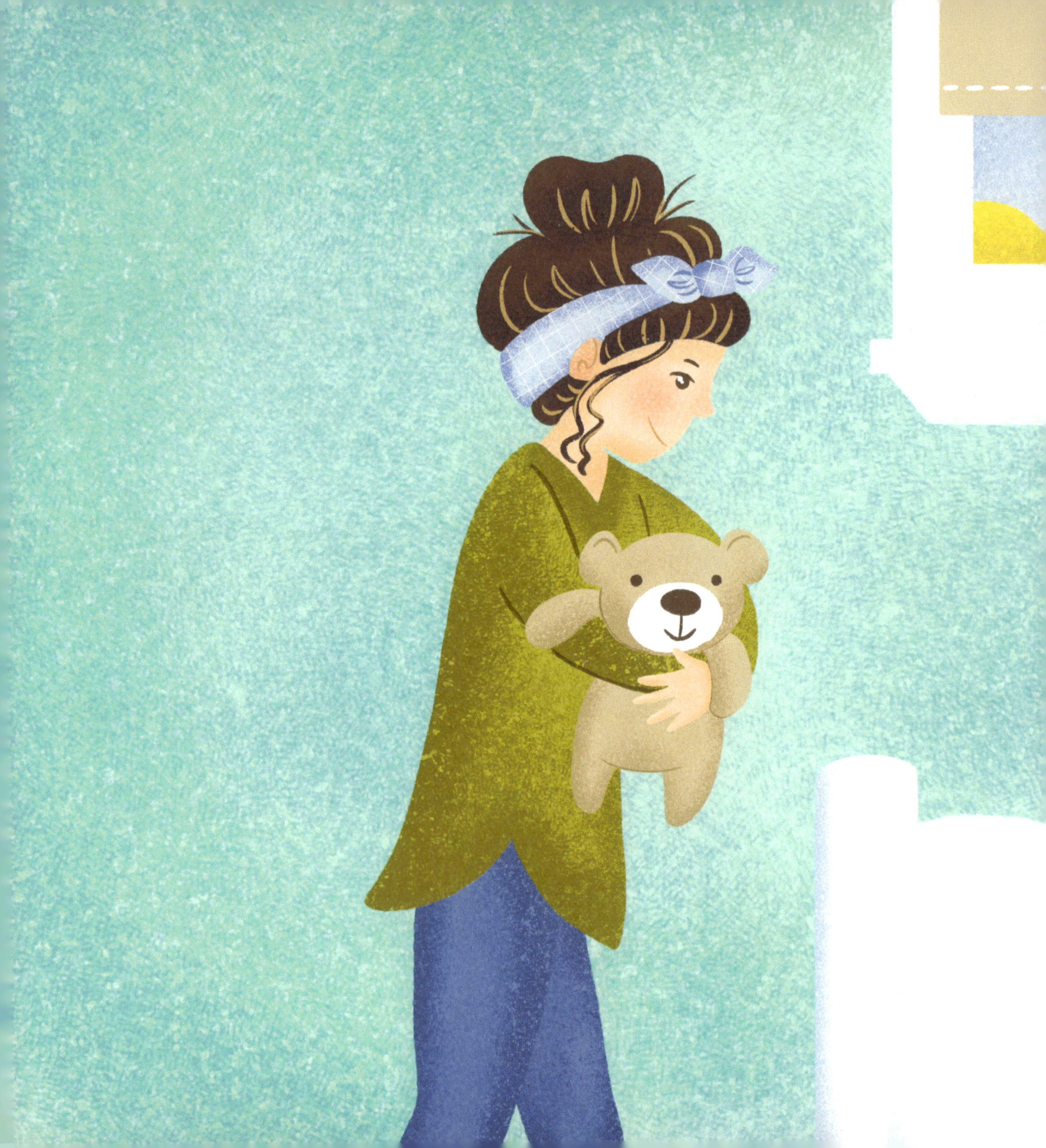

Okay, okay, I'll lie down
but these eyes
will not be closing.

I just like your back rubs.
I surely won't
be dozing.

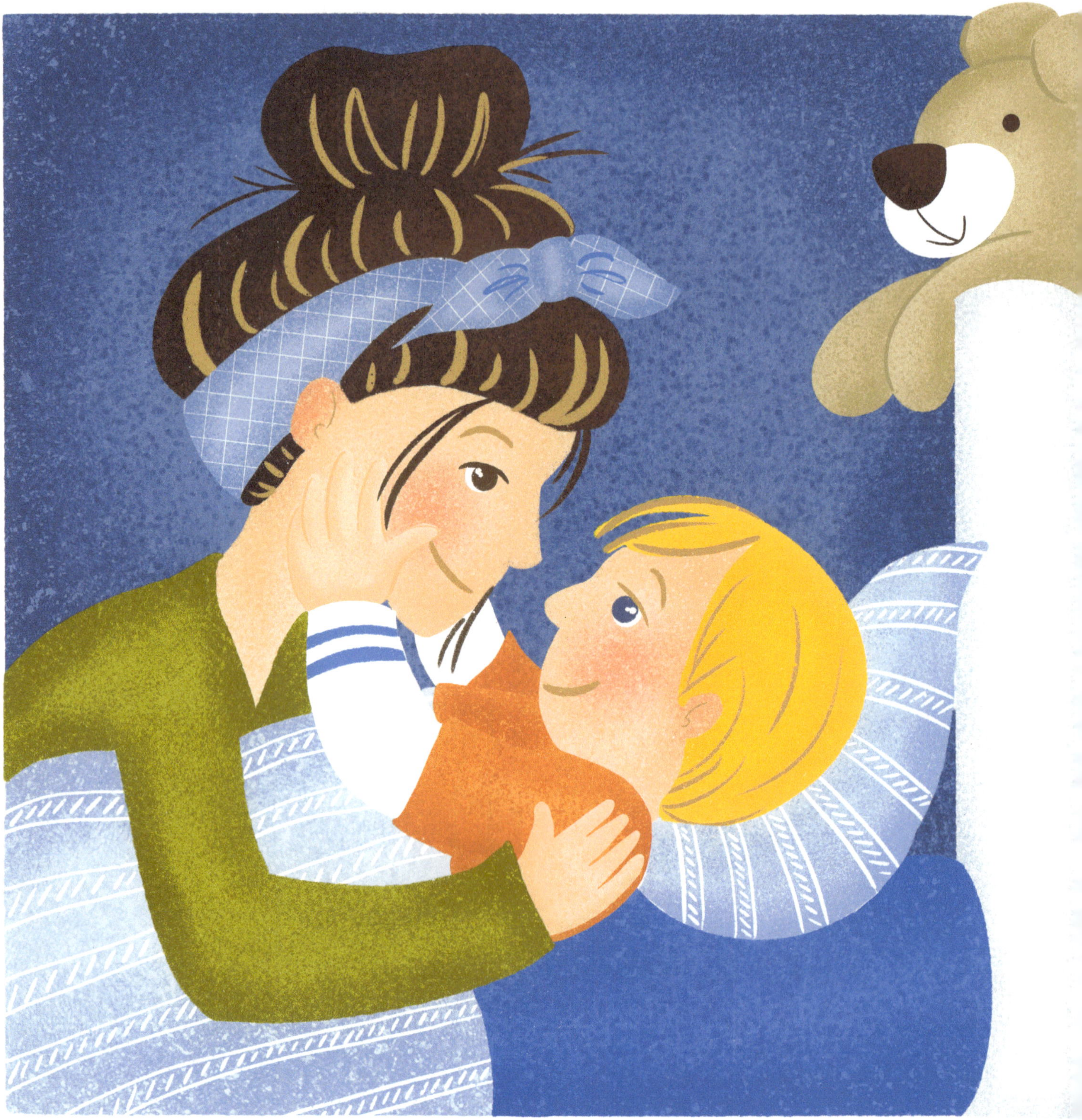

My heartbeat may be slowing down,
my lungs are breathing deep,

My eyelids are so heavy,
but I will not go to...

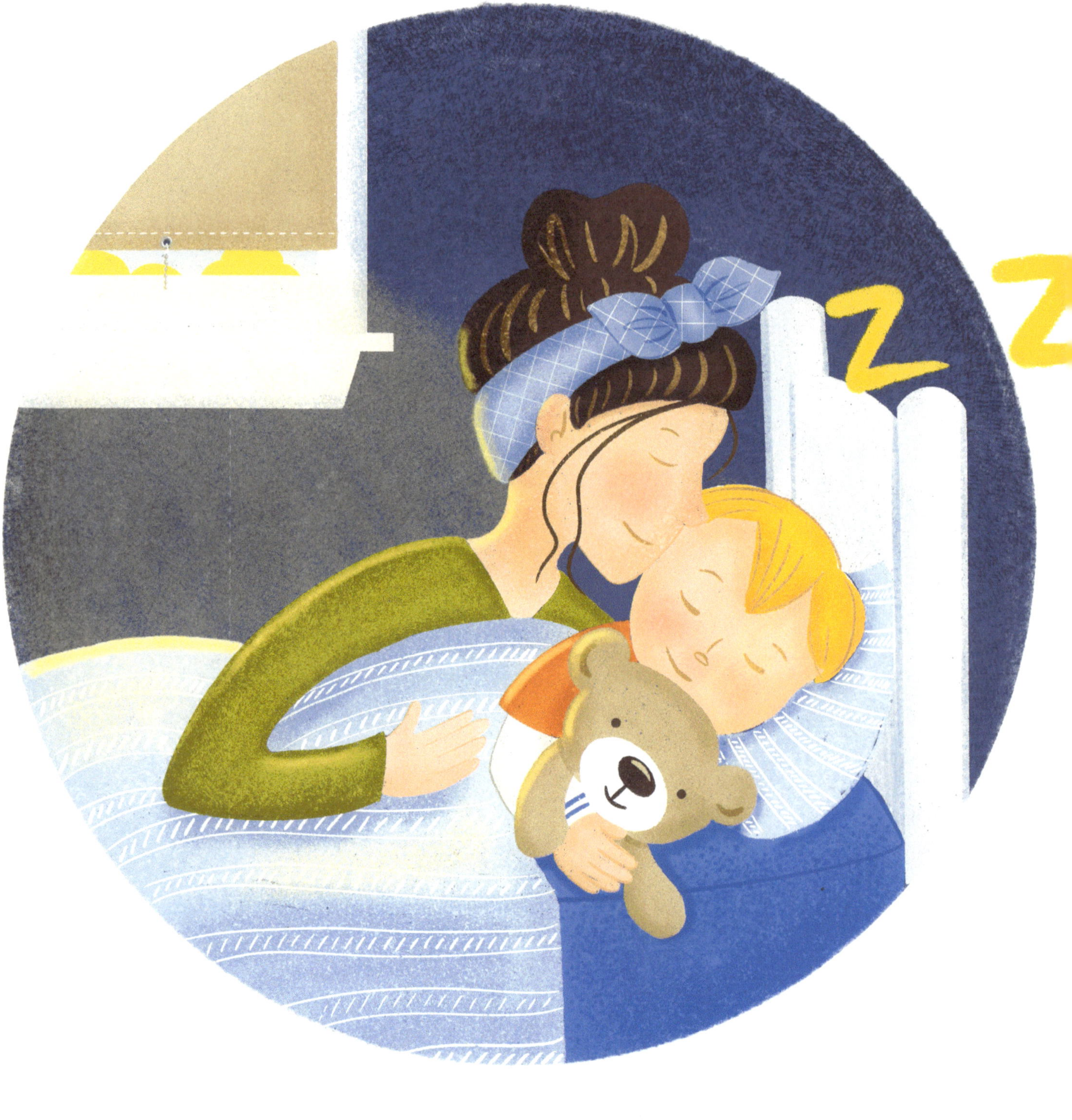
Z Z

Milton Keynes UK
Ingram Content Group UK Ltd.
UKHW051323080524
442321UK00010B/27